I0813478

ALSO BY SUNNYLYN THIBODEAUX

Curves & Curses (Auguste Press, 2000)
Last We Spoke (Auguste Press, 2004)
20/20 Yielding (Blue Press, 2005)
Room Service Calls (Lew Gallery Editions, 2008)
Palm To Pine (Bootstrap Productions, 2011)
88 Haiku for Lorca (Push, 2013)
As Water Sounds (Bootstrap Productions, 2014)
Universal Fall Precautions (Spuyten Duyvil, 2017)
Witch Like Me (The Operating System, 2020)
The World Exactly (Cuneiform Press, 2020)
Broadway Azaleas (FMSBW, 2024)

LUCKY CHARMS

CITY LIGHTS SPOTLIGHT SERIES NO. 26

SUNNYLYN THIBODEAUX

LUCKY CHARMS

NEW AND SELECTED POEMS

2000–2025

CITY LIGHTS
SAN FRANCISCO

Cover: Ryan Coffey, *In Advance of Lorca* (2009), 46.5" x 33", mixed media on paper [detail]
Cover photograph by Tate Swindell

CITY LIGHTS SPOTLIGHT
The City Lights Spotlight Series was founded in 2009,
and is edited by Garrett Caples.

ISBN 978-0-87286-945-5

Library of Congress Cataloging-in-Publication Data is on file.

The editor would like to thank Micah Ballard, Ryan Coffey, John Coletti, Carrie Hunter, Evan Kennedy, Jason Morris, and Tate Swindell for various forms of assistance.

City Lights Books are published at the City Lights Bookstore,
261 Columbus Avenue, San Francisco, CA 94133
www.citylights.com

CONTENTS

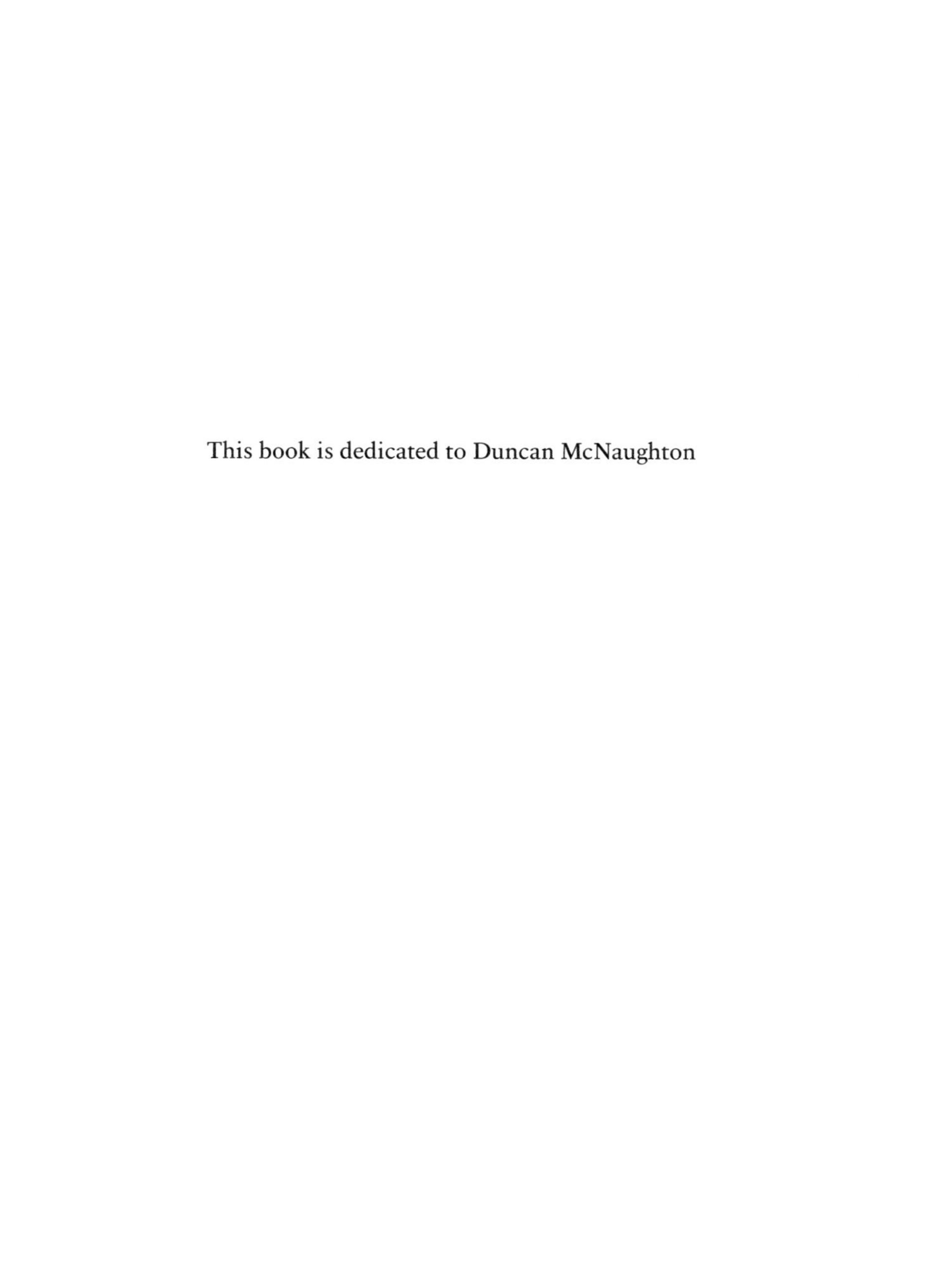

This book is dedicated to Duncan McNaughton

LUCKY CHARMS

LUCKY CHARMS

It is midafternoon. You are adrift
My head flutters with smiles of the dead
My heart aches. Rain let up
for a brief spell of warmth. More
to come tomorrow. Atmospheric river
sweeps in before we send it south, where
people are drowning sorrows in drink. Drunk
as a way of living. It could be midafternoon
when the sky shifts to slate, a banjo rips
A neighbor is dead. His smile keeps me
company in the process of grief. We prepare
for rain with buckets to catch the drops
from a grand hole up above. In the cloud
formations I can see his teeth and legs
He was all teeth and legs. It is midafternoon
There is a banjo. And a hole

SPRING BREED

At my mother's house
I pluck baby shoots of acorn
growth from her bed
of pansies and fair colored
periwinkles. She stuffs
artichokes in the kitchen
with potent garlic and parmesan.
I can smell the Italian
in her blood, stronger
than the trace of honey sweet
colored petals. I twist
the faucet knob, clockwise,
to let the water rush
over my hands and into
her weedless garden. I flood
the emptied soils and join
her for supper. She sets
a perfect blossom
of artichoke in the center
of the warped table
We sit and feast. She doesn't
mention the baby growing
in my belly or the mass
of mud under my nails. I pull a leaf
and drag it through my teeth

TULLULAH

And yet we return to the light that burns dim

The moon climbs walls
          scales of darkness, heavy night
all this silence and blood   torments for days
A crow casts a shadow on father's house
                    cries out like a child
the black beast of his soul
                    cries out like an infant

Slow down this tenderness
          torture with a crown
          dragging its monstrous feet
                    cross the South
          no seas, no hills

The temptress soars high above
          in beds of tulips   sleeps alone at night
          delves deep into pits of hell
                    wallpaper peeling down
               color of flames bursts through
she takes the crown of torture
               calls herself queen of this ridge
               sews it up inside her chest

gold thread, blackened heart

keeps the candles burning low
in case he needs to return

The woman has black eyes
all covered in inky drapes
I can't trust her to read
me—may be a drifter

These inhales have a tone
that may be the last or
a ball-out is coming on
hard—give me
your hands
just in case

de da da down
do de de dawn
da da de dis

slowly

ADONAI

The vinedresser's been at work
eighteen hours a day
                    pruning at ribs & fingers
                    stitching at my tongue

We don't surrender well
not even with a shovel
on the shoulder
                    gale force winds
                    mighty cypress down

you think it's someone else
then one by one the stars burn out

The desktop globe keeps
turning itself upside
down, squinting, South
America looks like a brush
of ash on the forehead

                    the silence of its spin
                    speaks volumes (starting with A)

20/20 YIELDING

the sign said
"Ahead at Church"
opened my eyes
quickly, quietly

often confusing
ocean view with
ocean beach to find
myself jumping
letters occupationally

to speak to someone
in case of emergency
red rain drops
graffiti seats
the SS in 4 minutes
Moses riding
the escalator down, approaching
1 car, Mission Bay
all I still long for

an empty seat
a thank you
a bottle of Hope & Grace

"IS IT TRUE YOUR FATHER WAS A SWAN"

before the sun
                has completely shown

I hang my head low
to be dipt in water
                        two times

add blueberries to my oatmeal
listen to a triangle chime
                                    an intermezzo

could sing you a melody
that wouldn't be my own
but the off pitch
        off chance   you'd recall

long have I waited
    a pot of jasmine tea (at 3 o'clock)
    an orange sliced ½ inch
    and an open hand
                        in anticipation of

"HIRED FOR THE PHANTOM"

FOR MICHAEL CARR

Trenton & Tex boxcars
stacked six sometimes seven
high, the green scape rolls
in lushness although the contra-
dictory train interrupts my view
I no longer see the Tyrannosaurus
in the sky, offshore winds
swallowed a seventeen-year-old
this morning walking the beach
in the dark
                    Softer White
with blue twine is today's read
the datebook nor the headlines
can compare. Lost between
the tokens of each page, I ride
the train longer than need be
somewhat south   century theatres
in the open door at Bay Fair, passing biscuit
and coffee manufactories. Heading
out the closing scene of *Point Break*
each of us hunts for shark teeth
in a sand box knowing there's no courage
to dive out at the Farallons

THANKS FOR THE TRANSIT FARE

FOR GREG FUCHS

our cross-town train barely
gets us anywhere, not as much as a double
Americano, more than the semicircle of the K
or M lines. Tawdry scenes overdone at night
special lenses so that I can find Andromeda
all the young artists
are tapping the atmosphere
but Kentridge is where my heart is
the promise of sunlight approaching
the memory of levee breaches
the here & now
isn't about us & them

"THE HOUR GROWS LATE"

a ruby grapefruit
is starting to mold
in the basket
                yo la tengo
                there's a fine background

sky blue sequins
are the great adornment
of your name-brand
handbag—didn't you
know
        there are six
new sunspots on each
shoulder & one awkward
shape on the cheek
        I don't know how
to talk about them
without curiosity

did you notice
        I ate the grapefruit

KISH-A-MISH

FOR LOGAN KROEBER

the straight blades of daffodils
holding out for spring, another
rain sweeps the roof

after the passing   turn to wwoz
for the family that runs the blood
Smiley Lewis and Fats
while drinking the peppery black
fruited syrah from the hills within

there are nine swallows stirring in figure eights
the jicama needs peeling twice, the radishes clean

put down your hands
so that I can see   Duncan calls
sending him home *Walking to New Orleans*
plays the ring

thinking hard through the sounds
left hand firm on the brow
the Alder flycatcher has an explosive fle bé-o
looking down   moles from my elbow to forearm
lead out to Pisces at October

METRY ASIDE

Looming with the legends
a post from an old friend, wearied by the dream,
reminds me to visit the cemetery on the first
somewhere between Mercury
& Osier   resting under broken thrones
ruins sat underwater white
stones & marble
stained an assortment
                              of earthtones
sorting thru yesterday's mail
this storm carves my calendar
hissing between August
and the next   the choir of precipitation
iron brush & directions in the left pocket
                              the stain of John Joseph
                              we take as a keepsake

SISTER MAYHEM

AFTER KATRINA

Count the hours
coastal erosion
up above, through & through
reflection of a false river
mirrors you

have you told your tale
of mothers laying ground
hands, graves proud
brothers disarming order

do you know
the assassins of this land
nameless faces unattended

you come here to confuse
mix up heart, dirty
with no reason
can you feel it, Armageddon

giant burdened beast, sister
give forth a sign
black and white
to smear on cheeks
warpaint of deathwater

do you wish to continue

awkward habits & quarry
dangerous then five days passed

I travel looking to find you
          surgical focus, characteristic sound
                              gargling winds
under my feet, on my back
in my ears   humming

to see the truth

chaos engine at last
with some idiot savant
slightly impressed

several breaches, 140 square miles
watermarks tattooed in script, vengeance
                    pledging to continue
                    dark waters, murky mouthed
we are silenced

double lick & strum
  landing end of summer
        & the radio reports

no regard, too heavy
scented, violent
please excuse us
there's a war to tend to
suits sneering

sister, I search for ways to forgive
unarrested regret roaming
waiting in line for this
refuse to forget
the string you plucked

dismember
in fields of grit & clovers & malevolence

you are given to ideal disgrace
with torture in your right hand
and death your left
touching from the distance
snicker as we struggle
with our posture, we are broken
toothed & still stand for an introduction

sister mayhem, let me tell you
I am Achilles and you
my enemy

MAJOR 5/6/7

Acacia, what is it you want
is it the same from near
as from far away

can you name it?

as Spicer says   death is
an image of syllables

do you hear it?

as Lorca says   if the dead
not close their eyes
they'd become swans

do you see   it?

as Whalen asks   it true
your father was a swan

do you know it?

Acacia, did you mean
to give all this

& what are we to do
with these words

write them
tell them
eat them alive

"HOW ALONE WE ARE THE MORE OF US WE KNOW"

FOR DUNCAN MCNAUGHTON

overtoned with riddles
        of imperious images

I was looking for a conversation
        of sailors & veils at birth
        (as my father had, some say)

        underneath the leaves, you found
        the key filmed in patina dust

I paid $17.99 for the Claret
you refused to drink, but
told you of the collection I stole
                silk & linen covered
                all letter pressed

your eyes sparkle (the color of whale skin)
in talk of Congo Square & brass bands
so I repeat myself just to see it again

everything in its right place
I feed you radio signals
and your response is   (cheers of a stadium crowd)
                "of course I will"

"THERE ARE NOT MANY KINGDOMS LEFT"

ON MY FATHER'S 68TH BIRTHDAY

it was sixty-eight years ago
        the songs that
        make my lips sound
        breaking in the new voice
near the tracks
near the Lutheran church
your sleep
        calms the sparrows,   in the evening
                        wakes the screech owl
we strike a dusty key   like lightening
there grew mushrooms in the trunk
                                a wet Schweggman's bag
light carpet muddied from some flood
you could blame me for stuffing
the street drains with pine needles and lost whites
so that a pool would form
in your eyes,   notes on nightfall
a symphony of June bugs beating at the porch light
rain prickling the pavement
this 31st is humid beyond repair
an unidentified protest
is withheld on the shore
                (what do we fear more the categories or the stages)
root up betrayal and a quince left to offer you
                                waiting here for the 4 o'clocks to bloom

FROM **ROOM SERVICE CALLS**

May I speak with Philip

I'd like
seedless watermelon
cubed, not balled
crumbled feta
and sunflower seeds

there is a melodic hum from the fan
complements the cloud coverage
83° today, eighty-three

do you have non-fat
do you have vitamin enriched

I am partial to Champagne
and pistachios

the choir of crickets
is cresting this moment

long distance phone-calls
are never worth the bill
when ballpoints are on sale

tell me about your mother

does the tv have a channel
that can be set to Joe Turner

the ice machine is low
not enough for the head
and the bended elbow

ga glunk

It has been hours, Philip
I mean days

tonight is clear
and the moon
almost full
in its glance
down this way

the scent of jasmine
could come through
this window, but
it doesn't open

the nose of the Alba
over the Asti
is more palatable

can we coordinate
the safe combination
to my favorite
songs. we can
use the radio dial

do you have an amenity
to pair with laughter

do you have laughter
or whole grain mustard

I have pretzels
Philip, do you have Damnation?

the roof doesn't
take me as high
as I'd hoped. can you
call a hot-air balloon

can I get out over
can I get over

there is a bad connection
the connection is bad

the dial tone doesn't sound
the way it used to

b-a-a-r-i-n-g
b-a-a-r-i-n-g

this is your wake-up call

but you
you are not Philip

HELLO, IT'S ME

FOR BABY BALLARD

There are just over a dozen
weeks left before we meet
Do you know me?

I wonder what your eyes will look like
Will they look like the sun?
Will your nose spread like the island?

Are you gonna expect me to sing?
Will I naturally speak in sing-song
tunes for your comfort?
Will you wake at 2 and at 3
and again at 4?

We have a small space for you
I think it'll be adequately comfortable
The walls are yellow and the woodwork dark
There is a large horse on the wall
I hope it brings you dreams of enchanted forests
and sandstone castles, notes from carousel songs

There are less than 100 days till your arrival
I am always planning with food
Do you agree with cheese
or heirloom tomatoes
sage and brussels sprouts
Will you be offended
if I have a glass of wine?

We do our best to save the planet
sometimes more so than ourselves
Will you take to this lesson
Will you share your pluots with the neighbor

Will your hair curl just on one side
your toes pick up a pencil?

When you meet me will it be what you were expecting
Will you know my scent, my crooked smile
How long will it take your eyes
to fix on my flaws?   your ears
to fix on the poem

Will you be in awe of the dragonfly
heartbroken by the sound of war?

When you learn our language
may thank-you be ever present
and translations of it abundant
        May you know the poem
        as a sound you can never turn off
        May you know this is only the first
        to welcome you into this broken world
May *it* be better for knowing your presence

FROM **AGAINST WHAT LIGHT**

Today's lesson is in synonyms
and dream retrieval

20:ix:10

It is silent
outside of the song
green & yellow light. We call out

in languages lost. 3 stories down
the streets gargle with the common
I can only write out in syllables

30:ix:10

Exit Music:

There are fragile things in the sky
All miners are above ground
They sent down the Virgin Mary with food
City Hall is orange
and the moon has gone from crescent

There were seven phone calls
with no one on the line
          my eyes focus on the noise
          my ears the touch
I just put your card in the mail
for appropriate timing. I liked
its humor. I like the mandolin
Each of the eight frames
on the wall slants right
I tried to return the call. I do believe
in ghosts. white noise. There are
fragile things in the sky

15:x:10

Today is Saturday, sky clouded over
Rain drops waiting for gravity to take them
Thirteen days   tyrant of grace
Belle & Sebastian serenading this phase
as it were ten years ago
                    the glorious moments of new relations
                    the awkwardness of learning to read each other
Thirteen days, as if it were always
forever learning changes
like water flow, not once

does it repeat itself. Not once
will we be here again

27:xi:10

The sky broken
with grey light. rain is predicted,
listen for breathing. I ask
her where her eyes come from
if she stole them off a traveler—
rare jewels from the banks of the Nile
curiosity & sorcery live there
sky changes
from dark to light, watch
perfection's chest rise and fall
It's 6:38 a.m. The war clouds
all waiting to turn

2:xii:10

The calla lily
was a gift for my labor
I've forgotten
to water it. The pillow
stained

with beets and supplements
of vitamin D
is a tell-tale sign
Tired of writing thank-you cards
Gazing into the ocean blue
the baldness of the sky
makes great light
against the mysteries
that're hidden there

6:i:11

Putin's touting revenge
Tens of thousands uproar in Cairo
Little babe in her Hendrix blue
drifts off to more peaceful lands
left side soaked while waiting
Giddy
about MacAdams on UNO, a post
to Duncan, roasted beets
I imagine the smash
of the television from three stories up
It blinks
Friends of the Urban Forest
have planted a Southern Magnolia
on the corner. I should

write them a thank-you
I should
write another post to a friend

26:i:11

Vague white,
a well defined storm
sits off the coast
carries rain for the weekend
In Patterson, two divers search
the murky waters to peer in
the windows of a Corolla

    what gives in what light
    against this white
    so many things have come undone

28:i:11

Timeless blue, 67°
spring comes early
so tells the creature
from his hole
half the nation

drenched in episodes
of cold white fury
          tonight will be moonless
          as people gather at the corner
          of orange street with well wishes
          and unspoken truths

2:ii:11

FROM **88 HAIKU FOR LORCA**

There was a shooting
Star on the day you were born
Here we go magic

*

House fly tapping glass
You have not seen this before
Exit determined

*

Get heliotrope
You must every time we pass
Sweet wedding cake scent

*

It's magic the way
Bubbles disappear when you
Catch them with your hands

*

Over the top and
Out of the crib you mastered
Stealth, agile ninja

*

There's so much to see
And so much to say. Your first
Sentence: *I see moon*

OUR TREASURES AREN'T EATEN BY MOTH

This is someone else's advisory
no more hushed by gravity than in humid times
clouds thick, choking the AM
there are no birds here, not in this hour
check them off our list
there are only compositions of puddles
running out to larger, a longing silence
not soon, nor suddenly
                    moment's suspect
                    raised on an elbow
                    climbing up, he comes down
it's long since someone's dime
stopped playing, where trumpets chorus
bullfrogs gossip in circles
among distant chiming voices
black drums thrusting on
                    the fish have eaten men
                    the sky has swallowed notes
                    an entire wilderness of freight
                    and private intimacies twelve heartbeats long
it would be things bloom
there in the field, under stones
burnt sprigs of fallen pines
          he's filled up on

by day stumbled red-eyed in the dust
the spark of sapphire isn't gone from the world
behind us, it is morning

ON LANDSCAPES/OF NETWORKS

come night
what song was
little come my way

The awaited dreamt
whether or not we
knew how or who—
we stood elsewhere
Shadows eroding
till we were spotted
and called out
what we behold

The underness has no place
an old release
tired of being sounded
song we'd like to be
called back as light
The loneliest host
free from them all
holds the night gone
sitting on the highest throne
the debris of watchtower acquaintances
finds shelter on & off the circuit

communing without nature
no one knew what to expect
everyone knew what was coming

KINGS RIVER CASTING

Waiting for the strong to take them
elsewhere, the romanticized version
of canals & barroom conversations is absorbed
in a biography of those unaccounted for
I am no bohemian, just modest
in remarkably unremarkable moments
The reserve is in the dialect of answers
to which route he took off Napoleon
we have often fared better from the lesser
ranks with magic as second nature
unconnected details whose gaps speak
loudly. This is a good town for dreaming
knowing Erik Weisz was the son of a rabbi

THE AWKWARD COLOR OF THE SKY AT ECLIPSE

It wasn't dark out
nor proper light
almost radioactive
                    hazy textures
                    a million miles off
                    not cornflower, nor orchard
                    more thistle, more electric

I've squandered the time
channeling propulsive energy
only to get inward
          thinking about how we've changed
          the ocean, floating islands of petroleum debris

The moon slid away
                    or was it the sun?
I couldn't look up
                    golden spent wavering about the floor

And I wonder what the birds must think
And I wonder how the fish complain

A DRESSING ROOM FOR DECATUR

To keep the untitled life off the mark
72 plates are made, 26 in color
halls echo with diagrammatic chatter
The strangeness of the familiar
gently pacing marble floors
The comfort of the strange lies in
an AM radio, the fact that
"Hell has frozen over, cher"
catching signals patterned as
the trembling of City Park lagoon
The United cab is stationary to checkmark
the occasion, sterling like a sound
that doesn't fit inside a single day
A beat isn't missed
St Aug could always choke me up
Picayune on round three and waiting
How did we come to stop here

LIGHT IN MY COUNTRY

the symmetry of light in my country
the symmetry of those passing through
            like a low trellis, unchanging among its dead
            these things of energy, all life
            with what water sounds as
            in the village, down the hallways
some exist parallel
a dimension higher & transparent
though it's been written
the shine is golden on the wall
like honeycomb dripping
            are those your footsteps
            falling off the sound of approach
            great heights, unknown reasons
            in the numbers, of twos
the symmetry of light in my country finds itself
breaking canopies, shedding signals
of twos, of twos, of
are those your footsteps falling off
ringing tones, last night, ringing circles
passing through the hallway
parallel in the village
are those your footsteps dripping golden
on the wall, as water sounds
the silence of symmetry approaching

THE VILLAGE WE COULDN'T ENTER

FOR SHAY ZELLER

Regardless where I was
I was somewhere else
so said nothing
stretch language so

There gave our blue
our grasp, our dreamlessness
reached in, picking up
to map and remap the shiftings
Where our feet have gone, tongues
tell tales. What was previous
grows out in our hair
the perfection we quest
whir of mystics

What critics we are!
checking boundaries
alternate worlds
over the drawbridge
just past the roar
of the train
where our feet have never gone
so said nothing
stretch language so

AND SO HERE WE ARE

Let us try
to convey the meaning of ambiguity
                    eliminate the visually disruptive
                    as if nothing matters
                    and all else does not
                    Interpreted conceptually

I have the tendency to talk
about the things most people won't
and so here we go
                    luminance
                    geometry
                    color
                    misc
                    setup

There are radionuclides in the water, Will

Can we replicate intensity?
Destruction as its own source material?
The absurdity of death is what I admire
most about you. This is not
a narrative. Quit yawning.
No one wants you to be comfortable

maybe salvaged, enriching, curiously basic
but not comfortable. It's the last place
any artist wants to be. So settle down
The compulsion to return is only just revealing
the leverage already within you

LIBRA IN THE IRISH CHANNEL

Everything that is placed here
all adds up to one
we got a letter stating a change in service
all specs in light & shadow
can drift too long in the escape
these strings are organized
into riverbeds & visible laughs
            six thirteen has housed many
            and homed those that won't move on
flash brilliant flash greenward
Lillian Russell in Vaudeville
but really it was 1953
glamour sealed inside
a descendant of voyagers
attack with love, respect outward measures
go ahead, ask the concierge

DOWN ON MULBERRY

The scatter of heritage
bundled up under root
        I could never pluck all
        those weeds, twisted
        and mud clumped
        baked into rocks

Such is hidden in all things
a name to carry
carved out in stone
        Don't think us telepathic
        just because we found you
        I have many questions
        and many notions

Once about drafting
go over again the line
and over again the blood
        Where fairness doesn't rest
        where titles don't either
        an arbitrary gesture—
        wooden box or ashen jar

You couldn't even dream
the stories we could tell
every vowel, mispronounced
            often mistaken race
            second language
My first name was his

TAKE ME BACK TO BARATARIA BAY

These are destroyers
left to make decisions in dark rooms
on the other side of the bridge
Sixty-two sunsets on slicks
no fix for worldly esteem
When we were optimists we dreamed
of pelicans and bald cypress
building cabins out of rain
The whole system is out of tune
and the floor has bottomed out
They are the translators of doom
the keepers of methane clouds
transfixed on monetary value
but the gallons have been all wrong
the moon'll never find its reflection in the dead
We stay up late waiting for retaliation
we stare out East watching the uprisings form

DEEP WATER HORIZON

It's been 58°
for days. I would need to take
a train to find a break of blue. Is
the same for the creatures of the Gulf
of Mexico

I've spent
lots of time thinking what to do
have no answers. press mute.
reflect on the pelican's grief, short off the list
the fishermen's empty nets
the service industry counting tips
the families still rebuilding
the watermarks still standing
frozen hours of the mess we're in

There is a jack
hammer outside my window. 2,000
miles away there is a junk shot, a top
kill, a CEO's transfer. Will we ever
have a shrimp po-boy again? The baby
doesn't even know it yet

Today, I won't
get out of bed. A city vehicle is in
reverse. Some Mexicans are on
the neighbor's roof, in my window
Por favor, señor, hay petróleo en el agua
and I am unsure what else to do

EVANGELINE, HOW DO YOU CALL YOUR TRIBE

FOR MICKEY SHUNICK

Down at the bayou the summer beamed on
no matter what news got my gut to pit
Small college town overgrown with haunts
of bodies tossed to swamp. Drowning
in chatter. A good year for hunting
I peddled the streets named for presidents and saints
past the halls I pulled my hair out in. Bike in the basin
Two fishermen spot black and gold. Late night surveillance
down to St. Landry   Charred out truck over the state line
What gets replayed in the head—sorted past, unregistered status
Ties to the year I left
Swamp deep bellow, rhythm of rain
It's not that I am. It's not like I know.
I could. I don't. I could be.
Thirteen-year lapse, not a likely drift
Frayed angels down the line
Bargained out disclosure, behind Claire Point
The hunt for a swamp iris
For a moment never quite right
rattled by a system
We don't dare breathe
We don't dare beckon
Between the flicker of light and the stars
This is the way back home

LAST NIGHT'S DREAM

I had French toast
with Tim Dlugos, his hands
trembling from meds
lenses reflecting back
at me myself. It was hard
to tell, but he spoke
sensical hand-me-downs
and that's how I knew—
like recognizing chords
in the newest band's rip-offs
skyrockets landing on hillsides
fresh whipped cream, strawberries
black coffee. done. with errors
on the page

FROM UNIVERSAL FALL PRECAUTIONS

Forgotten Monday
where all the words are lost on unread letters
that were mailed no matter
Grand satisfaction comes in assumed contact
whether rain or shine, sleet or hail

* * *

Dreamt I was a serial nudist
travelling atop public transit
through intersections. Captured
by non-color surveillance
The gossip was of a boy
I protested. Wanting
only proof of
the misinformation. Who
defines these categories?
femininity assisted
robotically to pathology
serial / surreal / sectional
surely surveillance
surely someone

* * *

Sometimes my love
misinforms me—

long holdout
for an outbound
All those coming and going
know not my burden
I wear it stitched along
the lower hem
They carry tales
carry curiosities relieved by gadgets
Misinformation
never a companion
Hair goes awry in the wind
as another train pushes in

***

Thirty-seven stairs in winter
meds running low
flashback to the cart
passing walled fluorescents, angels with nametags
pale green spin out that it was
gall bladder, navel, uterus
wakey wakey it's time

***

Note to self:
Don't move

INDEX NO. 3

FOR SARAH MENEFEE

As the dust settles
there's a machine, unmercied
falling. A glorious array of strangely
shifting takedowns breaking the already
broken. Where a circle starts   light
but revolted. Cornered.   We've been dead
here before but never quite in this variation
Unwound relativity, unalternating rise
All that's left is the shadow of liberty
picking at our pockets. Hollow particle
                                        Empty dust
Our voice is the only mortar left
and friends have all taken lodging
                                                elsewhere

INDEX NO. 39

Microscopic
locator
in case
of shift
right side
dense tissue
At the spa
darkened buttons
some bulleted
points, some
angle to the floor
for what I am
Nursery
Experiment
Time Bomb
Watch
move flawless
creatures sweat
troubles away
These troubles
carried under
imperfect skin
Sweat
they stay

Long since
the deductibles
Long since
the curve
of my back
led to satisfaction
Winter has
shaken down
all the leaves

ELECTRIC SYSTEM

We've got King tides
and Alice Coltrane sweeping
up the mood. It's Christmas Eve
and Japantown is overrun with littered
umbrellas and nitro puffs. Safeway smeared
with footprints and a Salvation
Army Santa playing a recorder
with his little red collection bucket. An emergency
landing at SFO. Rain is still pouring
through a hole in the roof. 94-year-old
landlord stopped in yesterday to say hello. *Shit*
came out when he saw the gape. *Get an estimate*
Rent hasn't been cashed making the account
seem inflated for delight. Santa Tracker
is running despite the government's
shutdown over a lack of empathy and an orange
man's temper tantrum. The spirit of giving
doesn't live in everyone. It isn't supposed to
Our shoulders are strong, and we will
continue to carry joy into the night
across borders of religion and race
because that one wish is the persistent hope
that we make it to know love in its
boundless array of faith. That we make it
to know love

WHAT BETTER TIME TO OPEN UP THE ZOHAR?

FOR DAVID MELTZER

Lorca's in the tub singing
about the rescue of America
in some gospel sounding croak
I'm staring at the framed Berman
image for *Luna*'s cover recalling how
it functioned as some sort of 12-step
program's guide during a bad run
How you chuckled with sincerity
and good tales of *bad runs*
of famed poets. Spinning
the light to assure I knew I was
in good company. I'd give a left
just to be Lamantia hiding from you
on the other side of the street
It would ensure that you're still here
and I could tell you of Lorca's songs
and how she views the world exactly
the way you would've taught her to

MEMORIAL DAY

All that's left is the shroud
                                                the back wings. Roaches
scurrying in the kitchen. There's no
greater threat than this time at hand
   Drunken cackles from the street. Still damp
                                                        from 4 AM rain
I missed the instructions for this part. The trap
Deflate of dream. Utopia was always
supposed to be right at hand. Right and left
Any which way we'd make of it
                                                          Marine layer
won't budge for the rumble under our feet. Sky
tears open in the north. Sirens
on high. A small pool forms
in the buckle of asphalt
In its gentle tremble
the reflection of the grey
white mass overhead
with a perfect seam of blue
The rift where
the dead speak
how-tos

MORNING SURVEY

My slanted ear
picks up a telephone's ring
not digitally compromised
but old school
bell and hammer dings
I can never tell the direction
from which sound travels
The monster garbage
eating truck swallows
all pleasantries
the preschool windchime gone
the sparrows' tweets
the notes of Belle & Sebastian through the screen
At some point
Threw a seed in a pot
It has since sprouted
but I cannot recall its genus
likely a lemon seed spit
from my water 3 years ago
It stands a foot tall
with its glossy green
leaves but can't really say
if bearing fruit is
in its future

A neighbor
put out a knife set
in its butcher block
orchestration along with
a box television and a sleeping bag
nearly making the street
inviting
How have we come to view
necessities as disposable?
How have we come to view
disposables as necessity?
The garbage monster ate
every thing in a series
of grumbles and crunches
and has moved
down the hill
Somewhere
in front or behind
left or right
a baby
is crying its heart out

BELLS ARE RINGING OUT/BIG FISH ODDITY

It's nearing 7 AM, sky is muted
with its moisture blanket. Spent
last hour with Kaufman's outlook
from the inside
of our less humanistic streets
although most are going by the same
name. Now with Tarkovsky. My heart bends
a little in compassion for lands
and times I somehow know
Rodney Reed's stay
is all the joy of this morning's coffee
with its cinnamon grit and oily drops
Dense fog advisory
won't lift for a couple more
rounds of hands. A friend lost
one of her babies in the womb
with 4 more weeks to go
while the brother readies himself
for this broken world. Could I
offer anything of comfort
in this white out morning?
A notebook and pen for grief letters to come
An embrace for the experience of receiving emptiness
Solace in children's nature of knowing

when spirits enter a room
Open heavenward
more than arms
and say a word
for the Scorpios
All arranging
and orchestrating chords
orange lights with dust
far off in the distant
realm of things we only know
when we're silent long enough
I've got your hand
here. His too. Sun
behind marine's cloak
Steam of coffee, cinnamon tint
Grief shrouds all hours of the day
no matter its fragile light. Hope
as a forgotten burning behind the sky
with its layers and palls and musicality

THE DEAL

The sunflowers have come
to bloom as we lay
our little bird down
There are sirens
on all edges
of this square—
anniversary of the quake
Chest quivers empty

Started these pots
seven years back
in a grieving process
for my unborn. Some
didn't pull through
bad air days. Some
stunted in growth. Some
shocked with a transfer

I wanted to save the bees
and ourselves
so went with flowerings
and herbs. Then someone
gave me a young lemon
tree treated with neonicotinoid

I felt relief
when it was stolen

My daughter wants another pet
I say, "give it time"
meaning, give *me* time
and re-water the shriveling
flower bed checking
for aphids and hungry caterpillars

CONNECTIVITY FROM THE OUTSIDE IN

FOR JASON MORRIS

Everything points to Desert Music. Dry brittle wind
Dry brittle posture. Siren at the mark of half day. Sun
doesn't peak for the trees. Fragmented light carried
in the ash of stirring
                                        In Iceland lava is spewing
from the cracks. The flanks of Bardarbunga
eyed with pressure, mystery. A moderate tempo. Heat
from within came without. Steam. Sulphur dioxide
Orchestrate
                                    The Creator Has a Master Plan
Known to cause respiratory problems. Dry brittle
wind. Magma pushing forth. We are part of it
Transcendence. Dainty feet. The mundane life
It has nothing to do with a rib. The flanks
The fissures. Summer something mountain top. Sub-
surface stream. There are white flowers on the water
Lava flowers on the water. Geologically
speaking, it could go any which way
                                                            Time tells
tales. They were said to be the first but Isha
was doomed from the get-go. The very best gift
comes from the heart

THE TRUTHS HAVE ALL BEEN CONVERTED

FOR LORCA BALLARD

A book was given from above
is how the story goes, one of the versions
of mans' knowledge. We come
from the earth in a way that is
different than their kind. Our knowing
spreads from a center
where nerve endings
cross in complexities—solar at least
Enoch as dismissed was likely not
a mother's decision. Raziel, keeper
of mysteries, may appear to reveal
things beyond our original scope
        The willow bends to form embrace
        The dandelion floats wishes to cracks & crevices
        medicines for many ails
        There are things to know
        as modes of survival
                (An army comes to land
                trumpets blast in afternoon sun
                                quick! retrieval)
There is an entrance and an exit
to every occasion, beginning and end
There are no hooves here, but fire
as mystery, magic and life

The things to know were always right here
Don't let them teach you beauty
as anything different
as anything the same
Be as quick as you may be slow. There is all the time
There is no time. In you
is everything already

SAINT JOSEPH'S DAY

I caught Frida Kahlo
over my shoulder
as I waited for results
at the doctor's office
Unsure what to make of
her company I treated myself
to a lesson in Japanese whisky
and pronunciation of Turkish
wines. My problems are likely
tethering. My problems likely
have histories. The rest of the
feelings were held in the curl
of my toes. Where else
were they to go. I spent a lot
of money in the shops. Thinking
about Frida and Reverdy and
Valrhona chocolate, a veil of health
as death rows on someone's shore

We all dress ourselves one last time

POWELL STREET, DECEMBER

These streets have a muted glisten
with its litter now stuck in the damp
A femme with extravagant lashes
stands cock-hipped in a wig cap
while she holds her locks
in one hand, she stuffs dollars
with her other into a peach satin bra
A bum at the corner
straddles a milkcrate
with a sogged sign
that reads, "Spread
the cheer. Spare change"
A millennial holds
up her cross-eyed company
as she eats a packaged danish
with its yellowed dough
Shoppers bust through
crowds with bags
that are no longer
free with purchase
A trolley grinds past
operator dinging a thudded Jingle Bells
Tourists beaming

at an open view
of a city that's lost
its love

TODAY'S POEM

The parakeet sings and chuckles from his cage
which needs a good cleaning. MRI results
were emailed before bed on a day the doctor
is not in. I feel I'm intelligent enough
to decipher good news in the mix. But I am
no scientist
                              My neighbor has let me know
she cannot make the building meeting
I scheduled to discuss our hopes of staying
housed as our landlord gears up for 95 and has
slowed in cashing our checks. Sometimes 3 months
at a time. One must be strategic in consumeristic
tendencies. Her grandfather traveled yonder
way out in Connecticut and she'll return when
all settles. Things may fall down before they settle
I want to tell her, but I offer assistance however I can
Blanket gestures are often overlooked. But worse is
blanket oversight—when people are too self-consumed
to acknowledge your struggle. They struggle with recon-
ciliation of their own needs vs the world
                                                                          The app
on the phone tells me rain will hold off for several more
days, but clouds will stick around. I want quiet time
to reflect on my health. Or to take hold of my health. Or

to quit thinking about complications of this life and the
number of days left to us. What would it look like
if we left this place. If I stayed high all the time
How would I change my perspective if the doctor
called with bad news again. How tired can one be
and still give it everything

FROM "Notes From The Fire Escape"

25. iii. 20

Gentle bees have come round
perusing mint, sage and thyme
I am lost in the apocalypse
There's a strong-armed man
in the clouds
a thousand insects
swarming fresh green leaves
of a Chinese elm below
Smoking neighbors stand
six feet apart shouting small
talk while I sit
thirty feet above on an escape
that is still too low
for the strong man to lift me

27. iii. 20

Black-headed hummingbird
sends electric chirps
in the wind
Children on scooters

dizzy themselves
in circles of safe distance
Pigeons squeak and coo
nestled on precipices
waiting on crumbs to
fall

7. iv. 20

There's a robin in song
on the MUNI line
under the pink moon
next to the blue building
south of Market

12. iv. 20

The retired addict downstairs
in his grey-toed white socks
and generic Fila slippers
complains about his diabetes
to a girl in pigtails drinking Korbel
straight from the bottle

13. iv. 20

Two children chase
their shadows
in pure excitement
to see each other

13. v. 20

Morning marine burned
off just after 8. Sirens
carried in the wind
Cumulus still hovering
over cranes' slow twirl
while helicopters float
over streets watching for
disturbances and headlines

FULL CIRCLE

In an effort
to support a future queer
I left a love note in a copy
of *Rubyfruit Jungle*
in a Little Free Library
next to the playground
where just I wanted to be
one of the boys

DELICATE AND BEAUTIFULLY PECULIAR

The azaleas are in
full bloom—an array
of pinks—from almost
white to a delicate fuchsia
Spring in the south
brings with it a yellow
dusting and caterpillars
that sting like
burning cigarette
cherries on cement

MORNING IN NOLA

An unkindness
of raven's cluck
and caw from
the empty branches
of the 100-ft-tall
water oak. Squirrels
won't leave their
hole for the brioche
torn about. Dawn
muted in January's
cold. Another ghost
crosses the open
kitchen window

DELTA'S GONE

Storm came bowling over
trees shed their dead
Electromagnetic rejuvenation
We are waiting
and waiting
for so many opinions to come
Opinions before remedy
Remedy before relief
How do we see ourselves
out of this particular hole
The heart sits there
I pick up branches from grass. Clouds
stack fluff and shift
Train bellows
Break stale bread
for the squirrels

THIS IS A NEW YEAR

I have drunk my mother's
coffee to the bottom a dozen
pounds now. Have trimmed her
holly and swept her roof
after each hurricane. I have
prepared electrolyte consumption
and protein in heavy rounds
but still I cannot cure her—herbs
for longevity—what more
is a daughter's role
where words are hard
to speak

ISOLATED SHOWERS

Sky's grey with the threat
of anticipated rain. Tap
overhead, wisp the five
foot sour weed. Beastly
charcoal movement
with its moisture collection
Twelve days till half
century mark. Dog days
they say, though I've lost
track of the stars in this
iteration. And I wonder
what Lew Welch would say
about these critters, these politics, this
crisis of climate. For many years
I thought I could be the one
to find him in the wood
since we are kindred spirits, Leos
and all. Wondered if his drinking
would bother me less
since being so enamored
by his poetry, the pain maybe
making sense, the encouragement
I could offer. Precipitation slaps the Blessed
Mother cracked at the shins under her robe

that I tried to freshen with paint
of my father's sixty-year-old
detail. Mildew and bare cement
cover the earth where her feet are
perched. A lizard on her shelter, invasive
species from some other
warm place, adapted quickly. Think
about planting a tree to find
shadow under, watch the birds hop
about trying to understand their placement
as scenery changes from old to new to old
again. Happy birthday season, dear Leo
Being lost is why it all started
to begin with. We could read Genesis
again, the serenity prayer, farmers
almanac. Storm moves on. Mosquito
hawks zoom across the St. Augustine
grass. There's a single drop still
dangling on the lily's blade,
pointing downward catching
light like a diamond

LET'S DRIFT

FOR KYLE SCHLESINGER

The collection of all
thoughts passing. Sun
trying to join company
of verse set with Anger's
Eaux d'artifice meditation
            "It's so good to see you"
The wind carrying
fountain's spray to mist
First of the notebook
scribbles—this one
woven red, gold cloth
glued with metal corners
A handout from a bodega
selling Sangria to-go
in Barcelona. It's felt intimidating
to write
            in something
            from an old city
            in something free
It's felt intimidating
to write. We break
through. Eventually
Like the sun that's
now on my shoulder

AUGUST 17

Sky fractured
with electricity
over the 3rd Baptist
over the Westerfeld House
Celebration, damnation
boundaries blurred
and defined as the mind's
rest wanes
Face seems the same
Some factions haven't
changed either, but
the world is on fire
Surely not on account
of me? Mother sings
a greeting, as in every
year. Father with his laugh
I don't write poems
to myself. Or maybe
they are all to myself
This day with
Sanders and Rivers
and the death day
of Spicer fantastique
If Billy the Kid could

hear us now. The radio
could tell us many things
if it weren't all lies
"Lady
of Guadalupe
Make my sight clear
Make my breath pure"
Poetry is my birthday
gift. Even better at forty-five

LENTEN SEASON

We're in a perpetual blanket
              of glaring slate, wasting
what the good lord has
                given us
after we complained
so.   Overflow rushing to
ocean. Catholics
              on kneelers
              in casual Sunday
                      best reciting
              creeds. Umbrellas
              gathered for
                          escort so
          as to not dampen
      the style. Newly risen

daffodils bending in the wind

THIS MUST BE THAT PLACE

FOR TIM COHEN

Pewter night
with vertical clouds

Mind's on Albion
and Atlantis

as if our destruction
came before our being

A Dadaist friend
never forgets the vibration

Invisibility comes in
many forms, but smallness

is the most concrete

WHERE DO WE GO FROM HERE

The first and only dead body I ever saw was when I was sixteen, old enough to drive, but not willing to do so. My mom chauffeuring me to my morning shift at the Häagen Dazs in the New Orleans airport. In front of the New Birth Cathedral of Glory near the city limit line, yellow tape and squad cars surrounded the intersection across from the levee. My mother told me not to look. And like all children when told not to do something, you do it anyway, as if the idea were actually birthed into existence by the instruction not to. I saw the sterile white sheet being draped ghost-like over skinny chocolate legs bent at the knee. The bottoms of the feet paler than the rest. The body was in the nook of brick where the cross tower protruded to the Crayola-colored blue sky scattered with tufts of cotton clouds. I wondered where God was in that moment. Was the victim as young as they were thin, my age even. If you die on a church's property are you promised to heaven? Every time I'm home I drive past the spot, now with my mother needing transport, still with questions in my head, about death, about life, about God, whether the river is high or low, will the levees breach again, how many years will I return here before I return forever. Death still abstract and visceral. Another diagnosis, another breath prayer, another storm. White crosses, golden crosses, hand-made crosses. Will all of our feet turn pale when we travel?

RENT CONTROL

The new neighbors
put out a feeder
for the sparrows and house
finches. We did this too
in awe of "wildlife" from
our city scape. Then came
the pigeons to make a home
Nests in the garbage
chute, on the ladder
the ventilation system
Eggs hatched, shit splatter
on every receptacle. They mate
for life you know. I want to
tell them that the building
is cursed. There was a fire
on the roof. A cat died
in their unit—Osiris. The elderly
teacher found comatose in their
bedroom celebrated many occasions
with us. There were bones
in the flower bed. An overdose
in the unit below. Once even,
Bobby Puleo and the Little People
band. There was a meth head

that threw his girlfriend out
the window, an ex-con hustler and a trench
coat smoker who didn't talk. There have been
dozens of 9-1-1 calls and a roof that leaked
for a decade. There may be mold. There may be
termites. Ants definitely find their way up
It's a good building. Neighborhood's
changed. No more gunshots, but I wouldn't
feed the birds. They tend to stick
around

NOTHING BUT FLOWERS

I wanted a different life
Dreamy different. More sun
More teaching. Less teaching
More transformative. Less war
Less politic. More hugs
More honesty. Less radiation
Less scary. More time
More sleep. Less toxins
More hikes, definitely more
hikes. Less ache. Less inflation
Less bullshit, definitely less bullshit
More dancing. More money, just a little
More synergy. Less technology
More birds. But the birds
keep on dying

ROUTINES

FOR MICAH

The morning air holds
the rumble of cleaners
Ravens strut through shadows
collecting spilled debris
No Look Backs!
as I am pulled to the Jesus
Freak pamphlets at the free
library and you are calculating
the weight of the world in your mind
Sky has a haze but more blue
than grey. I scan the return of Christ
language for similarities and try
to catch a glimpse of you up
the hill. Met with glare from windshields
as the sun rises a little more. I wave
into the light just in case

SIGNS OF LIFE

Rush hour at the crosshairs
like a modern-day Fellini film—
ledge of the 16th street subway
system bustling with handshake drugs
chatty frequenters, chihuahuas and pitbulls
A thin man in a hoodie nodded
out his fix while straddling his 3-speed
Head near his waist, bendy straw curved
spine, bike still upright like a magic trick. Sun
shifting lower casting shadows for long
patterns, basketry weave design
of the Pomo people. From a corner
hand-held radio the agile voice
of Maria Callas giving everyone chills

AL-SHIFA

FOR PALESTINE

Fluorescent grey was required
if any else remained
There were trees of phonics
and castles burned into stardust
The sea foam whistled Berlioz
or something like it from the heart's tear
It was ceremony in most cases
traditions and formalities
The emptiness swallowed everything
There isn't even death when everything is gone
There isn't even death. Forever
watching people rise and float
The sky imperfect all the way to the sea
Forever. The sea and its requiem

THERAPIST ASKS ME TO DESCRIBE GRIEF

Storm comes like Gorgon slither
Gorgon wingspan

Sound is someplace else
like head under water someplace

Tumbling, duckweed cover, under water someplace
Where is Eurydice
Is that echo

These walls never ending
These walls anonymous navigation
We crossed, we did indeed
We crossed looking for the spirit
of the storm
Lapping tides exed out winds lavender in all

Earth bound is what comes
bound by forces of dark
forced dark

Heaven's spread thinned out
universal texture of gum
universe mugged

the ground's bottomed out
            outed, muddied as all hell

The heart caught in the grey clouds moving

I AM WITHOUT

There's a metallic purple peel
of fingernail polish
on the fake Persian rug
and I realize, again, for the eighth
time before noon, that my mother
is gone. My daughter flecked
her proud paint job off while sitting
on the sofa, one finger at a time
in a nervous handling of space
as she half-listened to me talk
about some parenting
connection I desperately wanted
I recount all the times
my mother snapped
in my direction as I nervously
gnawed at each tip
Never purple or metallic
hued knowing the chemicals
would end up in my mouth
and I was a conscientious worrier
I'm drawn to that tendency as
I stare at the other lost fragments
designer and culinary alike
strewn about the mahogany

and grey-leafed tapestry
knowing that I should vacuum
for a tidier space. I should vacuum
to rid this homey display
of the broken pieces
of things forgotten
overlooked glitter
and cookie crumbs. After all
it is what mothers do
but I am without
and it all seems so dear

THE COLLECTIVE INDIVIDUAL EXPERIENCE OF DROWNING

RECOLLECTION ON KATRINA 20 YEARS LATER

They say a front
is keeping things at bay, quiet
for this anniversary. My daughter
asks why I sound like that when I recall
things. Sound like there's a frog
in my throat, Spanish moss, sheetrock. Sound
like the caked cracked mud that covered the land
has filled my voice box. There's water
trying to get held back
in my eyes, slowly a trickle comes forth
She says, I don't like when you talk about it
because you always cry. You weren't
even there! I wasn't there. I wasn't there. Out
in Cali hanging around a silver keg
for a fundraiser for dogs. Friends asking,
so how bout this storm? Sparks in
the eyes. Fear, curiosity. Unbothered
breath, my family knows
what to do. Evacuating is for wusses. We've
got a grill, beer, clawfoot with ice. Went
to bed secure. It was six
days before I knew
where my mama was. Her younger sister

actually forced her out as they went
on their way. Gridlock. Contraflow. Brake
light red parade. They got
to Alexandria. To Natchitoches. Bounce
holiday hotels. No cell service. Network
gridlock like Christmas tree string lights tangled
after you ask the kids to take them down. It was six
days. The news repeated images of neighbors with the most
desperate expressions on rooves, on
knees, waving flags. Help Us. Saviors
in pirogues and flat bottoms. 15 feet. 9 feet.
12 feet. 8 feet. Watching, standing in a private
puddle. Hoping to catch a glimpse of my own
neighborhood, my NanNan's neighborhood, a recognizable
face showing signs of life. Dead
bodies float. Cars on fences. Houses
off the foundation. I hunted
through each repeated image of epic
failure. Hunted channels for differences, online
forums for familiar names. I hunted
and waited the longest waits, picked
up smoking again, until the phone
rang for every single one of them

MAILBOX FULL

I want to say you're on my mind in all the hours that I cannot call. It's 2:13 AM and some weird wiring of my system woke me. My mind running through a to-do list and on that to-do list is "catch-up" with all the people that I love so that they know that I love them. I want to tell them that I'm struggling with the loss that has piled, but I don't want to make it about me. I just want connection and to not feel regret when you go. But that is making it about me again. I'm struggling with that part. This shit sucks. Grief and all. Whatever the mess of this complication is. It isn't cut and dry. But I wouldn't say all that on a voicemail. I promise. I would just say that I miss you and that you are on my mind. Often. I mean I wouldn't call often. I'd just let you know I am thinking about you often. But I would call often if you'd like. And if I had time. Time isn't friendly when you're trying to grieve. Or just figure shit out. It just keeps going with no regard. And there's bills past due and a new appointment and some scheduled evening meeting I'm too tired to remember and then it's like, oh hey when's the last time you talked to your friend? Oh yeah, I should do that because I want them to know that I love them and because frankly this grieving shit is super lonely, but I don't want this to be about me. So I wouldn't ever say that. But really, I love you. That's all I want to say, but your mailbox is full. I'll try again. I won't wait so long. I'll try again soon I promise. When I get a moment to actually breathe

ACKNOWLEDGMENTS

Variations of poems have been previously published in a variety of print and online magazines. Tremendous gratitude to each and every one of those editors for choosing this work to feature: *Arts Fuse*, *As of Late*, *Big Bell*, *Boog City*, *Castle Grayskull*, *The Dust Never Settles*, *Duende*, *Poetry Magazine*, poetryproject.org, *Spirit Duplicator*, *Touch the Donkey*, *Trampoline*, *Pure Paragraphs* for Kevin McNamee-Tweed's art show "Pilcrow" at Dutton in New York, and the anthology *Cuneiform@25: A Retrospective* (Cuneiform Press).

Nothing happens without community, on and off the page. I would like to thank the magicians for orchestrating the sensibilities as they do in their own work and, as always, for the feedback: Chris Ashby, Jeff Butler, Micah Ballard, Sarah Cain, Ryan Coffey, Christina Fisher, Jason Morris, Ryan Newton, Rod Roland, Kyle Schlesinger, Nick Whittington, Will Yackulic, and James Yeary. I am also forever indebted to the selfless brilliant editor Garrett Caples who made this opportunity possible.

The state of the world calls out for poetry to save it. LAWRENCE FERLINGHETTI

CITY LIGHTS SPOTLIGHT SHINES A LIGHT ON THE WEALTH OF INNOVATIVE AMERICAN POETRY BEING WRITTEN TODAY. WE PUBLISH ACCOMPLISHED FIGURES KNOWN IN THE POETRY COMMUNITY AS WELL AS YOUNG EMERGING POETS, USING THE CULTURAL VISIBILITY OF CITY LIGHTS TO BRING THEIR WORK TO A WIDER AUDIENCE. IN DOING SO, WE ALSO HOPE TO DRAW ATTENTION TO THOSE SMALL PRESSES PUBLISHING SUCH AUTHORS. WITH CITY LIGHTS SPOTLIGHT, WE WILL MAINTAIN OUR STANDARD OF INNOVATION AND INCLUSIVENESS BY PUBLISHING HIGHLY ORIGINAL POETRY FROM ACROSS THE CULTURAL SPECTRUM, REFLECTING OUR LONGSTANDING COMMITMENT TO THIS MOST ANCIENT AND STUBBORNLY ENDURING FORM OF ART.

CITY LIGHTS SPOTLIGHT

1 Norma Cole, *Where Shadows Will: Selected Poems 1988–2008*

2 Anselm Berrigan, *Free Cell*

3 Andrew Joron, *Trance Archive: New and Selected Poems*

4 Cedar Sigo, *Stranger in Town*

5 Will Alexander, *Compression & Purity*

6 Micah Ballard, *Waifs and Strays*

7 Julian Talamantez Brolaski, *Advice for Lovers*

8 Catherine Wagner, *Nervous Device*

9 Lisa Jarnot, *Joie de Vivre: Selected Poems 1992–2012*

10 Alli Warren, *Here Come the Warm Jets*

11 Eric Baus, *The Tranquilized Tongue*

12 John Coletti, *Deep Code*

13 Elaine Kahn, *Women in Public*

14 Julien Poirier, *Out of Print*

15 David Brazil, *Holy Ghost*

16 Barbara Jane Reyes, *Invocation to Daughters*

17 Carmen Giménez Smith, *Cruel Futures*

18 Edmund Berrigan, *More Gone*

19 Uche Nduka, *Facing You*

20 Sophia Dahlin, *Natch*

21 D.S. Marriott, *Before Whiteness*

22 Evan Kennedy, *Metamorphoses*

23 Roberto Harrison, *Isthmus to Abya Yala*

24 Patrick James Dunagan, *City Bird and Other Poems*

25 Thea Matthews, *GRIME*

26 Sunnylyn Thibodeaux, *Lucky Charms: New and Selected Poems, 2000–2025*